Plant Top Tens

# Africa's Most
# Amazing Plants

www.raintreepublishers.co.uk
Visit our website to find out more information about Raintree Books.

To order:
☎ Phone 44 (0) 1865 888112
📄 Send a fax to 44 (0) 1865 314091
💻 Visit the Raintree Bookshop at www.raintreepublishers.co.uk to browse our catalogue and order online

First published in Great Britain by Raintree,
Halley Court, Jordan Hill, Oxford OX2 8EJ,
part of Pearson Education.
Raintree is a registered trademark of Pearson
Education Ltd.

Produced for Raintree by Calcium

Editorial: Kate deVilliers and Sarah Eason
Design: Victoria Bevan and Paul Myerscough
Illustrations: Geoff Ward
Picture Research: Maria Joannou
Production: Victoria Fitzgerald

Originated by Modern Age
Printed in China by South China Printing Company

ISBN 978 1 4062 0967 9
12 11 10 09 08
10 9 8 7 6 5 4 3 2 1

British Library Cataloguing in Publication Data
Scott, Michael and Royston, Angela
  Africa. - (Plant top tens)
  581.9'6
A full catalogue record for this book is available from the British Library.

Acknowledgements
The authors and publisher are grateful to the following for permission to reproduce copyright material: ©Alamy Images pp. 6 (LOOK Die Bildagentur der Fotografen GmbH), 7 (TBKmedia.de), 23 (Diomedia), 24 (Images of Africa Photobank); ©Corbis p. 21 (Nigel J. Dennis/ Gallo Images); ©FLPA pp. 12 (Peggy Heard), 20 (Wendy Dennis); ©Istockphoto pp. 4, 8, 15 (Jan Roode), 22; ©Natural Visions p. 26 (Colin Paterson-Jones); ©Nature Picture Library pp. 18 (Martin Gabriel), 25 (Jim Clare); ©NHPA pp. 9 (Ar Eckart Pott), 14 (Ann & Steve Toon); ©Photolibrary pp. 13 (Garden Picture Library), 27 (Botanica); ©Science Photo Library p. 19 (J M Downer); ©Michael Scott pp. 10, 11, 16, 17.

Cover photograph of a baobab tree, reproduced with permission of Alamy Images/Andy Rouse.

Every effort has been made to contact copyright holders of any material reproduced in this book. Any omissions will be rectified in subsequent printings if notice is given to the publishers.

# Contents

Some words are printed in bold, **like this**. You can find out what they mean on page 31 in the Glossary.

# Africa

Africa is a huge **continent**. The vast Sahara **Desert** covers the north of the continent. The Namib Desert is in the south-west. In between are high mountains, **rainforests**, and grassland. African grasslands are called **savannahs**. Deserts, savannah, and rainforests are different **habitats**. A habitat includes the plants and animals that live in a particular place.

## Climate

A **climate** is the kind of weather a place usually has. Most places in Africa have warm climates. Deserts are very dry because very little rain falls. Other places are wetter.

Savannah is grassland with a few trees. Many animals live on the savannah, including herds of gazelles.

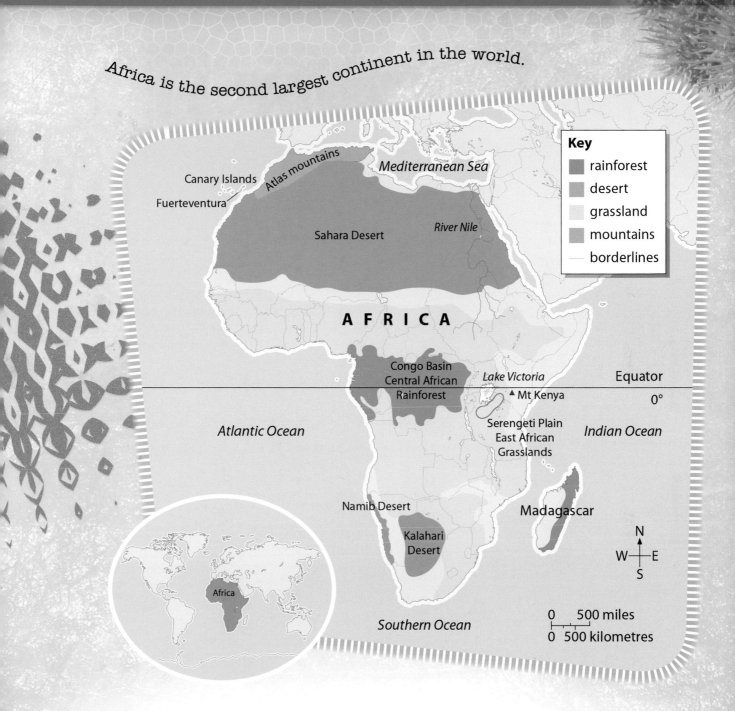

**Key**
- rainforest
- desert
- grassland
- mountains
- —— borderlines

Canary Islands
Atlas mountains
Mediterranean Sea
Fuerteventura
Sahara Desert
River Nile

A F R I C A

Congo Basin
Central African
Rainforest
Lake Victoria
▲ Mt Kenya
Equator
0°

Atlantic Ocean
Serengeti Plain
East African
Grasslands
Indian Ocean

Namib Desert
Madagascar
Kalahari
Desert

Africa

N
W—E
S

0    500 miles
0  500 kilometres

Southern Ocean

Many plants grow best in the rainforest, where it is
warm and wet all year round. In Africa people have
cut down most of the rainforests to make farmland.
Few plants can grow in the desert, where it is very dry.
High mountainsides are very cold and windy, so few
plants grow here, either. Some plants have amazing
ways of surviving in these difficult habitats.

# Baobab tree

The baobab tree grows on the savannah. It is called the "bottle tree" because its thick trunk is shaped like a bottle. A baobab is filled with water! When it rains, its roots suck up water. The tree stores the water in its trunk. Some baobabs are so fat it would take 15 to 20 people holding hands to reach around the trunk. During the dry winter season, the tree slowly uses up the water and its trunk becomes empty.

### Water store
People who live in the Kalahari Desert drink water from the trunk of the baobab. They use grass **stems** as straws.

Baobab trees become so big because they keep growing for hundreds of years.

## BAOBAB

**HEIGHT:**
UP TO 25 METRES (82 FEET)

**LIFESPAN:**
AT LEAST 1,000 YEARS

**HABITAT:**
SAVANNAH

**THAT'S AMAZING!**
ONE BAOBAB TREE WAS SO WIDE THAT A SMALL ROOM WAS CUT INTO ITS TRUNK. IT IS USED AS A TINY PUB OR EATING PLACE.

where baobab trees are found

**Africa**

Atlantic Ocean

Indian Ocean

Southern Ocean

People often meet in the shade of a baobab tree.

## Upside-down tree

Baobabs are sometimes called "upside-down trees". This is because their branches have leaves for only a short time in summer. For the rest of the year the bare branches look like roots. All trees lose water through their leaves. A baobab saves water by dropping its leaves.

# Welwitschia

Welwitschias are amazing plants that grow in the Namib Desert. It hardly ever rains here, but the desert is often covered by mist or **dew** at night. Like all plants, they leak water through tiny holes in their leaves. But welwitschias can also soak up water through these tiny holes. They use this trick to take in water from the mist and dew.

## Leaves

Unlike welwitschias, other plants lose their leaves from time to time. Trees with broad leaves often lose all their leaves in winter. **Evergreens** lose their leaves too, but not all at the same time.

Each welwitschia plant has only two leaves. They become split, tatty, and tangled in the desert wind.

## Precious water

The welwitschia's two leaves grow from a thick stem. The stem is up to 1.5 metres (5 feet) wide. The root reaches deep into the soil, searching for precious water. Many of the plant's **seeds** are eaten by animals. The rest may lie in the ground for many years until it is wet enough for them to start growing.

The woody cones on this welwitschia plant each contain many seeds.

### WELWITSCHIA

**HEIGHT:**
UP TO 50 CENTIMETRES
(20 INCHES)

**LIFESPAN:**
400–2,000 YEARS

**HABITAT:**
DESERT

**THAT'S AMAZING!**
THE WELWITSCHIA MAKES ONLY TWO LEAVES IN THE WHOLE OF ITS LIFESPAN.

where welwitschias are found

**Africa**

Atlantic Ocean

Indian Ocean

Southern Ocean

# Jandia spiny spurge

The Jandia spiny spurge grows on Fuerteventura. This is a hot, dry island off the west coast of Africa. The plant can survive here because it stores water in its thick stem. The stem of the plant is protected by long, sharp spikes. Each spike is up to 3 centimetres (just over 1 inch) long. The spikes stop animals from eating the stem.

When it rains, the Jandia spiny spurge takes in water and stores it in its stem.

## JANDIA SPINY SPURGE

**HEIGHT:**
UP TO 1 METRE (3 FEET)

**LIFESPAN:**
PROBABLY MANY YEARS

**HABITAT:**
DESERT

**THAT'S AMAZING!**
JANDIA SPINY SPURGES ARE HARD TO FIND. THIS IS BECAUSE THEY GROW ONLY ALONG A NARROW STRIP OF COAST ON THE SOUTHERN TIP OF FUERTEVENTURA.

where Jandia spiny spurges are found

Fuerteventura

**Canary Islands**

Atlantic Ocean

**Africa**

# Holding on to water

The spines are actually leaves and they help the plant to save water. Most plants lose water through their leaves, but the Jandia spiny spurge loses very little water. This is because each spine has only a very small **surface area.**

Jandia spiny spurges grow on dry, rocky ground where few other plants can grow.

## Succulents

A Jandia spiny spurge is a type of **succulent.** Succulents store water in their stems or leaves.

# Stone cactus

These tiny plants grow in a stony desert where it hardly ever rains. They look like stones, but their leaves are full of water. Stone cacti are succulents. They are so well disguised that even thirsty animals pass them by. They look like plants only after it rains. Then two brightly coloured flowers quickly grow between their leaves.

Stone cacti look like pebbles in the stony desert.

### Photosynthesis

Green plants make their own food. Their leaves take in the gas **carbon dioxide** from the air. The gas joins with water in the leaves to form sugar. The energy for this process comes from sunlight.

# Leafy window

Some stone cacti have a **transparent** (see-through) window at the tip of their leaves. This lets sunlight into the leaf. Like other green plants, stone cacti use sunlight to make their food. The process is called **photosynthesis**.

The flowers of the stone cactus look like daisies.

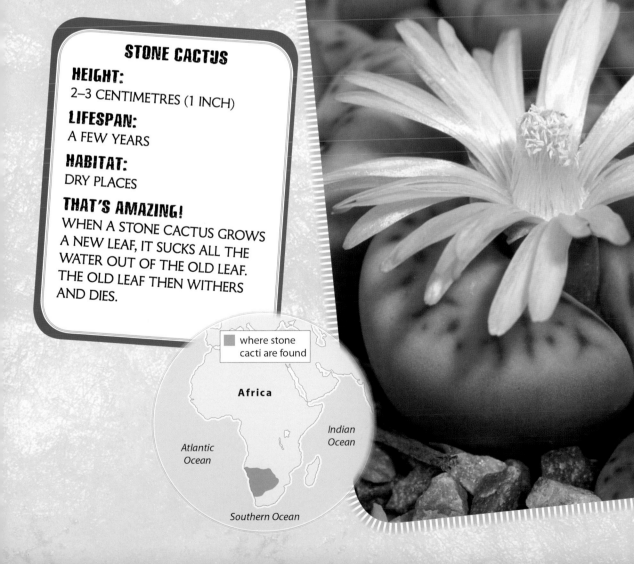

## STONE CACTUS

**HEIGHT:**
2–3 CENTIMETRES (1 INCH)

**LIFESPAN:**
A FEW YEARS

**HABITAT:**
DRY PLACES

**THAT'S AMAZING!**
WHEN A STONE CACTUS GROWS A NEW LEAF, IT SUCKS ALL THE WATER OUT OF THE OLD LEAF. THE OLD LEAF THEN WITHERS AND DIES.

where stone cacti are found

Africa

Atlantic Ocean

Indian Ocean

Southern Ocean

# Karoo gazania

Karoo gazanias grow in the west of South Africa. For most of the year the land is brown and dry. It rains only in spring. Then, all at once, the ground is covered with great masses of flowers.

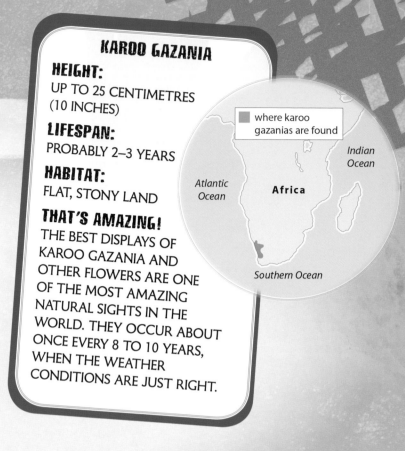

**KAROO GAZANIA**

**HEIGHT:**
UP TO 25 CENTIMETRES (10 INCHES)

**LIFESPAN:**
PROBABLY 2–3 YEARS

**HABITAT:**
FLAT, STONY LAND

**THAT'S AMAZING!**
THE BEST DISPLAYS OF KAROO GAZANIA AND OTHER FLOWERS ARE ONE OF THE MOST AMAZING NATURAL SIGHTS IN THE WORLD. THEY OCCUR ABOUT ONCE EVERY 8 TO 10 YEARS, WHEN THE WEATHER CONDITIONS ARE JUST RIGHT.

where karoo gazanias are found

Indian Ocean

Atlantic Ocean

Africa

Southern Ocean

The beautiful flowers of karoo gazania last just five weeks.

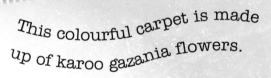

*This colourful carpet is made up of karoo gazania flowers.*

## Return of the dry season

When the dry season returns, the land becomes brown again. The plant shrivels up and its leaves become dry. This stops the plant from losing water. The dead leaves help to protect the plant's underground stem from the hot sun. When it rains again the next spring, new leaves and flowers quickly grow.

# Parasol lily

A parasol lily grows from a **bulb**. After it rains in winter, the bulb grows a few tough, narrow leaves. The leaves soon dry up when summer comes. It is dry all summer so the plant lives on the store of water and food in its woody bulb.

The flowerhead of a parasol lily is made up of 100 or more tiny flowers.

## PARASOL LILY

**HEIGHT:**
UP TO 45 CENTIMETRES (18 INCHES) TALL

**LIFESPAN:**
30 YEARS OR MORE

**HABITAT:**
DRY, FLAT, STONY GROUND

**THAT'S AMAZING!**
THE BULB OF THE PARASOL LILY IS POISONOUS. THIS STOPS ANIMALS FROM DIGGING INTO THE GROUND TO DRINK ITS STORE OF WATER.

where parasol lilies are found

Indian Ocean

Africa

Atlantic Ocean

Southern Ocean

# Flower ball

**Wildfires** start easily during the hot summer. A wildfire burns the plants but not the bulb, because it is safe underground. Soon after the fire, the bulb produces a tall flowerhead with many tiny flowers. When the flowers have made seeds, the flowerhead dries up and breaks off. It forms a ball that rolls in the wind, scattering seeds as it rolls.

This burnt ground has been cleared of plants. It is perfect for seeds to grow in.

# Dragon tree

Dragon trees grow in dry, rocky places. Their long roots grow deep into the soil to search for water. Goats and sheep eat the leaves of any young dragon trees they can reach. Today most dragon trees grow high up on rocky cliffs. Hungry animals cannot reach them here! The plants can grow here because their long roots anchor them to the cliff.

This dragon tree is growing on the island of Madagascar, off the east coast of Africa.

# Dragon's head

The trees get their name because they sometimes look like dragons from a distance. The big bushy branches look like a dragon's head. The scars on the trunk look like scales on a dragon's neck. People call the plant's red **sap** "dragon's blood".

## Sap

Sap is like blood to a plant. It contains water, sugar, and other **nutrients** the plant needs. It flows through narrow tubes to every part of the plant.

When the trunk or branches of a dragon tree are cut, red sap oozes out.

## DRAGON TREE

**HEIGHT:**
UP TO 18 METRES
(60 FEET)

**LIFESPAN:**
OVER 600 YEARS

**HABITAT:**
DRY, ROCKY
PLACES WITH
RICH SOIL

**THAT'S AMAZING!**
THE ANCIENT EGYPTIANS USED THE SAP OF DRAGON TREES MIXED WITH OTHER INGREDIENTS TO PRESERVE THE BODIES OF DEAD PEOPLE. THIS IS HOW THEY MADE MUMMIES.

Africa

Indian Ocean

■ where dragon trees are found

Madagascar

# King protea

King proteas grow in places that are dry for part of the year. The surface of the leaves is thick and leathery. This stops them losing water. It also stops insects and other animals eating them. The leaves are so hard they snap if you bend them.

These king proteas are growing on Table Mountain in Cape Town, South Africa.

## KING PROTEA

**HEIGHT:**
UP TO 3 METRES (10 FEET)

**LIFESPAN:**
SEVERAL YEARS

**HABITAT:**
HEATHLAND

**THAT'S AMAZING!**
THE KING PROTEA'S BEAUTIFUL FLOWERS ARE UP TO 30 CENTIMETRES (12 INCHES) ACROSS. THAT IS BIGGER THAN A DINNER PLATE.

where king proteas are found

Africa

Atlantic Ocean

Indian Ocean

Southern Ocean

A cape sugarbird picks up pollen when it sips the flower's sweet juice. The juice is called **nectar**.

## The king

There are 115 different types of flowering protea. The king protea's flower is the most splendid. Cape sugarbirds use the dried petals of the flower to build their nests. They also carry **pollen** from one flower to another.

# Castor bean

The castor bean plant grows especially well in land that has been ploughed or dug. That is because it is very good at spreading its seeds. When the seeds are ripe, its spiky red **seed pods** explode! Thousands of beans are scattered in all directions. Inside each bean is a seed and a store of food. The seed uses the food to grow into a new plant.

The flowers on a large castor bean plant can produce up to 150,000 beans.

## CASTOR BEAN

**HEIGHT:**
USUALLY 3–5 METRES (10–16 FEET) BUT CAN BE 12 METRES (40 FEET)

**LIFESPAN:**
SEVERAL YEARS

**HABITAT:**
GRASSY PLACES AND PLOUGHED LAND

**THAT'S AMAZING!**
JUST 60 GRAMS (2 OUNCES) OF RICIN COULD KILL A MILLION PEOPLE.

where castor beans are found

Africa

Indian Ocean

Atlantic Ocean

Southern Ocean

# Deadly poison

Castor beans contain a deadly **poison** called ricin. The poison stops animals from eating the beans. Ricin is very strong. Eating just three castor beans would kill a person. When the beans are crushed, however, they produce castor oil. This has been used as a medicine for thousands of years. The poison is removed from the oil.

# Giant lobelia

Giant lobelias grow on the high slopes of Mount Kenya. They have much taller flowers than the other plants that grow here. The mountain is on the **Equator**. The Sun is fierce during the day, but the nights are very cold. The giant lobelia uses its feathery leaves to avoid freezing to death. At night it folds down its leaves to cover the flowers. This keeps the flowers warm.

The giant lobelia has many small flowers. They are hidden amongst its fluffy leaves.

leaves

# Liquid anti-freeze!

The giant lobelia has another trick to stop it freezing at night. Its long, hollow stem contains a slightly sticky liquid. This liquid never freezes, however cold it is outside. It keeps the plant warm from the inside.

GIANT LOBELIA

**HEIGHT:**
2–3 METRES (6–10 FEET)

**LIFESPAN:**
PERHAPS UP TO 100 YEARS

**HABITAT:**
HIGH MOUNTAINSIDES

**THAT'S AMAZING!**
GIANT LOBELIAS FLOWER ONLY ONCE, THEN THE PLANT DIES.

This colourful sunbird reaches through the leaves to find pollen. It carries the pollen from one flower to another.

where giant lobelias are found

**Africa**

**Mount Kenya**

*Indian Ocean*

*Atlantic Ocean*

*Southern Ocean*

# Plants in danger

Many plants in Africa are in danger of becoming **extinct**. A plant is extinct when there are none of its kind left in the world. One reason that plants become extinct is that their habitats are destroyed.

Swartland sugarbush is a kind of protea. At one time there were just four of these plants left growing in the wild. Much of the land where these plants used to grow has been turned into farmland. Many other plants were eaten by animals or destroyed by wildfires.

Swartland sugarbushes are becoming more common again because scientists have planted many new ones.

African violets are very rare in the wild because people have collected so many of them to sell.

Scientists try to save plants that are in danger of dying out. They grow them in special gardens or greenhouses. Only a few African violets still grow in the wild. But African violets are very common house plants. There are now 40,000 different types of African violet that are grown as pot plants.

# Plant facts and figures

There are millions of different kinds of plants growing all over the world. The place where a plant lives is called its habitat. Plants have special features, such as flowers, leaves, and stems. These features allow plants to survive in their habitats. Which plant do you think is the most amazing?

## BAOBAB

**HEIGHT:**
UP TO 25 METRES (82 FEET)

**LIFESPAN:**
AT LEAST 1,000 YEARS

**HABITAT:**
SAVANNAH

**THAT'S AMAZING!**
ONE BAOBAB TREE WAS SO WIDE THAT A SMALL ROOM WAS CUT INTO ITS TRUNK. IT IS USED AS A TINY PUB OR EATING PLACE.

## WELWITSCHIA

**HEIGHT:**
UP TO 50 CENTIMETRES (20 INCHES)

**LIFESPAN:**
400–2,000 YEARS

**HABITAT:**
DESERT

**THAT'S AMAZING!**
THE WELWITSCHIA MAKES ONLY TWO LEAVES IN THE WHOLE OF ITS LIFESPAN.

## JANDIA SPINY SPURGE

**HEIGHT:**
UP TO 1 METRE (3 FEET)

**LIFESPAN:**
PROBABLY MANY YEARS

**HABITAT:**
DESERT

**THAT'S AMAZING!**
JANDIA SPINY SPURGES ARE HARD TO FIND. THIS IS BECAUSE THEY GROW ONLY ALONG A NARROW STRIP OF COAST ON THE SOUTHERN TIP OF FUERTEVENTURA.

## STONE CACTUS

**HEIGHT:**
2–3 CENTIMETRES (1 INCH)

**LIFESPAN:**
A FEW YEARS

**HABITAT:**
DRY PLACES

**THAT'S AMAZING!**
WHEN A STONE CACTUS GROWS A NEW LEAF, IT SUCKS ALL THE WATER OUT OF THE OLD LEAF. THE OLD LEAF THEN WITHERS AND DIES.

## KAROO GAZANIA

**HEIGHT:**
UP TO 25 CENTIMETRES
(10 INCHES)

**LIFESPAN:**
PROBABLY 2–3 YEARS

**HABITAT:**
FLAT, STONY LAND

**THAT'S AMAZING!**
THE BEST DISPLAYS OF
KAROO GAZANIA AND
OTHER FLOWERS ARE ONE
OF THE MOST AMAZING
NATURAL SIGHTS IN THE
WORLD. THEY OCCUR
ABOUT ONCE EVERY 8
TO 10 YEARS, WHEN THE
WEATHER CONDITIONS
ARE JUST RIGHT.

## DRAGON TREE

**HEIGHT:**
UP TO 18 METRES
(60 FEET)

**LIFESPAN:**
OVER 600 YEARS

**HABITAT:**
DRY, ROCKY
PLACES WITH
RICH SOIL

**THAT'S AMAZING!**
THE ANCIENT EGYPTIANS
USED THE SAP OF DRAGON
TREES MIXED WITH OTHER
INGREDIENTS TO PRESERVE
THE BODIES OF DEAD
PEOPLE. THIS IS HOW
THEY MADE MUMMIES.

## KING PROTEA

**HEIGHT:**
UP TO 3 METRES
(10 FEET)

**LIFESPAN:**
SEVERAL YEARS

**HABITAT:**
HEATHLAND

**THAT'S AMAZING!**
THE KING PROTEA'S
BEAUTIFUL FLOWERS ARE
UP TO 30 CENTIMETRES
(12 INCHES) ACROSS.
THAT IS BIGGER THAN
A DINNER PLATE.

## CASTOR BEAN

**HEIGHT:**
USUALLY 3–5 METRES
(10–16 FEET) BUT CAN
BE 12 METRES (40 FEET)

**LIFESPAN:**
SEVERAL YEARS

**HABITAT:**
GRASSY PLACES AND
PLOUGHED LAND

**THAT'S AMAZING!**
JUST 60 GRAMS
(2 OUNCES) OF RICIN
COULD KILL A
MILLION PEOPLE.

## GIANT LOBELIA

**HEIGHT:**
2–3 METRES (6–10 FEET)

**LIFESPAN:**
PERHAPS UP TO 100 YEARS

**HABITAT:**
HIGH MOUNTAINSIDES

**THAT'S AMAZING!**
GIANT LOBELIAS FLOWER
ONLY ONCE, THEN THE
PLANT DIES.

## PARASOL LILY

**HEIGHT:**
UP TO 45 CENTIMETRES
(18 INCHES) TALL

**LIFESPAN:**
30 YEARS OR MORE

**HABITAT:**
DRY, FLAT, STONY GROUND

**THAT'S AMAZING!**
THE BULB OF THE PARASOL
LILY IS POISONOUS. THIS
STOPS ANIMALS FROM
DIGGING INTO THE
GROUND TO DRINK ITS
STORE OF WATER.

# Find out more

## Books to read

*Animals and Plants*, Andrew Langley (Oxford University Press, 2002)

*Plant Life Cycles*, Anita Ganeri (Heinemann Library, 2006)

*Plants and Planteaters (Secrets of the Rainforest)*, Michael Chinery (Crabtree Publishing Company, 2000)

*The Power of Plants*, Claire Lewellyn (Oxford University Press, 2005)

*The World's Largest Plants*, Susan Blackaby (Picture Window Books, 2005)

## Websites

www.junglephotos.com/africa/afplants/afplants.shtml
Click on photographs of African plants.

www.junglephotos.com/africa/afscenery/afscenery.shtml
Information on the habitats of Africa.

www.kidsgeo.com/geography-for-kids/0153-biosphere.php
Learn more about weather, habitats, and how plants survive in them.

www.mbgnet.net/bioplants/adapt.html
Discover how plants adapt to different habitats, including deserts, grasslands, tropical rainforests, temperate forests, tundra, and water.

www.plantcultures.org
Find out about plants from all over the world at
Kew Gardens' website.

www.wildwatch.com/living_library/plants-1
Find out more about the amazing plants of Africa.

# Glossary

**bulb** round part of a plant from which new stems and leaves grow

**carbon dioxide** one of the gases in air

**climate** the kind of weather that a place usually has

**continent** large area of land that includes many countries. There are seven continents in the world.

**desert** place that gets very little rain and has few plants

**dew** drops of water that form on cool surfaces overnight

**Equator** imaginary line around the Earth at its widest point

**evergreen** plant that has green leaves all year round

**extinct** no longer in existence

**habitat** place in the wild where particular types of plant grow and particular types of animal live

**nectar** sweet juice made by flowers

**nutrient** part of food that is needed for health

**photosynthesis** process by which plants make their food using the energy of sunlight

**poison** something that is harmful if eaten or touched

**pollen** grains of yellow dust made by flowers

**rainforest** forest where it rains almost every day and where plants and trees grow close together

**sap** plant juice made mainly of water and sugar

**savannah** in Africa, a wide area covered in grass with few trees

**seed** part of a plant that can grow into a new plant

**seed pod** closed pouch that contains seeds

**stem** part of a plant on which leaves or a flower grow

**succulent** plant that stores water in its stem or leaves

**surface area** the area of the surface of an object

**transparent** see-through

**wildfire** fire that starts by accident in the wild and is difficult to put out

# Index